THE
JOY
OF BEING GAY

A Gay Christian Handbook

Thomas Krahn

The world's leading gay biblical theologian

ISBN 978-1-0980-9774-5 (paperback)
ISBN 978-1-0980-9775-2 (digital)

Christian Faith Publishing
832 Park Avenue
Meadville, PA 16335
www.christianfaithpublishing.com

All scriptures quoted come directly from the Authorized Standard King James Version of the Bible: a book that the Protestants have held in reverence for over four hundred years.

Printed in the United States of America

CONTENTS

CHAPTER 1

The Joyous Gay Manifesto

I will praise thee; for I am fearfully and wonderfully made:
marvelous are thy works: and that my soul knoweth right well.
—Psalm 139:14

Come let us celebrate our masculine sameness. Let us revel in our virile oneness. Let us take joy in our muscular arms, in our well-wrought legs, in our solid torso, and in our manly buttocks. From our heads to our toes, let us take joy. We are the Adams, the first causes, the namer of animals. And we are all alike.

Even though there may be a million variations of us, we are still alike, the same yet different.

Some of us are tall; some are short. Some are muscular, yet some are lean.

But we are all males, men endowed with nature's blessings of manhood, hanging down between our legs. And all the time, our marvelous bodies are creating more of the male elixir, constantly reinforcing our maleness.

All of nature sings with us. It invites us into its treasured realm of first causes. We are created to be our own alpha and omega, our own beginning, and our own end. Did not God create man from the earth and breathe the miracle of life into him?

We are part of nature, and nature is part of us—an unbreakable bond.

I choose to remain there in the treasured realm of first causes. I, myself, am part of man, and I wish to remain with other men, never once brutalizing my primal sensitivity. I am intact and content to remain, so no matter how many men I might choose to share my maleness with, I give my body to them while they give their body to me. As we share our feelings together, we intertwine as only the sameness can experience.

I am gay, and I thank the God that made me as a first cause. To Him, I repair when the forces of doubt and despair arise. I will not fear. For did the Creator of all first causes not stand ready to comfort me with His reassuring love and compassion? Did He not say He would be with me in all ways?

I can spread my naked arms and embrace the skies!

I am complete, yet not complete. Whole, yet lacking—looking to complete my sameness with another sameness of the first cause.

And what a meshing of maleness that will be—the sameness coupled with another sameness in mutual embrace.

It is my body. It is my choice. It is my choice who I share my maleness with, and not anyone else's. I will not use my wonderful masculinity to breed with. Animals do that, and I am not an animal. I am a human being, self-conscious, and aware of my body.

It is the only thing that is really mine.

There are other things, but they are only material possessions that someday others will own. But no one can ever own my body. Whether they confine it, shackle it with chains, or cause it pain, it still remains uniquely my own.

Yet even then, I only have it for a little while. After I leave my body, there is no other spirit that can own it as I have owned it. And it will eventually crumble to dust as the Scripture says in Genesis 3:19, "In the sweat of thy face shall thou eat bread, till thou return unto the ground; for out of it wast thou taken: for dust thou art, and unto dust shall thou return."

But though I have it for only a short time, I will revel in its wonderful dimensions. I shall inhabit my whole being, from the bottom of my toes to the top of my head.

And with my body, I can be anything I want to be. I can be macho, leading armies, conquering nations, and commanding thousands. Or I can be a poet, a musician, or an artist tuning into the rhythms of nature. I can caress a rose, and yet with that same hand, I can crush it.

I can live in the grandest palace or a lowly hut. It is my home, and no one else's. I can make it a warm and friendly house with Louis XIV furniture and crystal chandeliers or a cold, unwelcoming dungeon with benches and hard chairs and weaponry hanging on the walls. It all depends on what I want.

I can play football or knit prayer shawls. I can play baseball, yet sew quilts. I can play soccer, yet create a beautiful nocturne by Chopin on my piano.

It all depends on what I want to do with my body. I am gay. If I choose to wear leather and chains, it's okay. Just as dressing in drag is all right. Or I can choose to wear conventional clothes—that's acceptable too. Whatever I choose to wear, it's my decision to make and not anyone else's.

In fact, I can choose to wear nothing!

That's okay, for there are places where I can go and openly display my maleness for all other males to see. And they can also choose to display theirs to me.

We can openly see the sameness, the maleness, even though there are a thousand variations. There is nothing hidden. Even if we try to be coy, our wonderful bodies give us away. There is no hiding physical interest in one another. When we are truly interested, our bodies will show it. And quite visibly.

Yet we need not feel guilty. We are celebrating our manly oneness. We are the Adams, the first causes, the namer of animals. We are gay, and nothing can take that away from us. We are created in His image. And in His image, we shall forever remain.

CHAPTER 2

The Joy of Definitions

Define your terms and I will gladly debate with you.
—Attributed to Voltaire

One of the big problems with discussing gay people and gay expressions is the lack of terminology. This was caused by the Roman Catholic Church for almost a thousand years. Pope Urban II (circa AD 1075) started the campaign against us, and it has persisted almost to this day. It was a campaign of total condemnation and silence. No one dared to talk about the subject of same-sex existence and marriage.

If you did have those *unnatural* feelings, you were expected, under your own volition, to lie among the bundles of wood laid at the feet of a heretic who was to be burned at the stake. And then you were expected to be burned to death with him. From that came the term *faggot*.

Even when Martin Luther broke from the RCC, the Catholic thinking about gay life moved right over to Protestant thinking.

That twisted thinking even spilled over into business and government. And it has remained there for hundreds of years until someone actually picked up the Bible and read it through gay eyes. Now things are beginning to radically change. Terms like *fairy*, *faggot*, *homo*, and *queer* are no longer acceptable.

That is why new terms must be used or old terms redefined to include same-sex relationships. The first term we will look at is the term *homosexual.*

Shere Hite, in her very well-researched book on male sexuality, wrote, "Homosexual should never be used as a noun, but only as an adjective describing certain sexual acts." In other words, a man should never be called a homosexual or *homo* in the common parlance. To do so would only qualify him by his sexual acts.

To prove my point, there are many men who commit homosexual acts, such as prisoners, many men away at sea for an extended length of time or any situation that would include men being isolated together for a while. They may commit homosexual acts with each other but quickly revert back to heterosexual activities when they return to society.

There are also many men who indulge in homosexual acts for any number of reasons: they get no sexual satisfaction at home or are simply curious.

In either case, the man in question is not gay. He is locked in the birth-life-death cycle of the straight life. In most cases, desiring a wife, children, and fatherhood. He may occasionally stray into homosexual acts but never remains there for too long.

The gay life is simply not his cup of tea so to speak.

But then what is gay?

Gay is a different way of looking at things. We are not encumbered with the past even though we might embrace it. Even though we might live within societies' dictates, we are not entrapped in its straight jacket.

We are quick to innovate when the occasion calls for it. A good example is the "twist." Legend has it that it was invented in a place called "The Peppermint Lounge." In there, men were not allowed to dance together, and so the twist was born.

On a personal note, I was the first one to wear Bermuda shorts in my hometown. It caused quite a scandal until the other men realized it was more comfortable wearing short pants rather than long pants. Now you can see men in shorts all over the place. Some of the more daring ones even go so far as to wear very short shorts.

Another example is the pink twisted piece of ribbon worn on the lapel. It was originally black and stood for the victims of AIDS. That, until the women took it over, turned it pink and had it stand for women's rights.

I'm sure the reader himself can call to mind other instances where it was the gay person who improvised something new that the straight people have picked up and made their own.

It becomes very evident at this point that being gay is a lot more than sexual acts. Unfortunately, all too many of us have made it the sum and substance of our existence.

The straight people have ridiculed us for our *barnyard morality*. Yet how many of them could still function morally after having been condemned by the church, thrown out and almost destroyed by the military, scorned by society, and cast out of their families? Very few!

Thank goodness the universal condemnation, for the most part, has stopped. We are not accepted yet. At this point, we are only tolerated.

Yet despite these conditions, most of us gay people go on to lead productive and rewarding lives. Why there is a gay man with his husband in plain sight, who actually ran for president.

And he is not ashamed of being gay as his opponents would have him be.

Oh yes, we do have sex. All human beings are blessed with sexual urge. But we must be very careful to practice safe sex.

Saint Paul writes in 1 Corinthians 6:18, "Flee fornication. Every sin that a man doeth is without the body; but he that committeth fornication sinneth against his own body."

And Saint Paul's practical solution to his admonition to flee fornication?

> But if they cannot contain, let them marry: for it is better to marry than to burn. (1 Corinthians 7:9)

The ancients knew what venereal disease was and how it was transmitted.

A faithful gay marriage solves one big problem, if it is a problem, right off the bat. And it can be a solution as soon as both parties realize they can't go to bed with every cute guy in town.

One complaint of gay marriage is that there are no children. But as gay people, we are not here to reproduce the race. Our extra time, money, and energy are to be put to good use, producing spiritual children.

What are spiritual children?

Every tree a gay person plants, every poem he writes, every song he composes and/or sings, every whale he helps to save: these are all examples of our spiritual children.

As we shall see, God has a special place for us. That is why we must try, as hard as we can, not to misuse this wonderful blessing of gayness. He gave it to us for a very special reason.

Even the prophet Isaiah tells us to be happy.

> Sing oh barren, thou that didst not bear;
> break forth into singing, and cry aloud, thou that
> didst not travail with child. (Isaiah 54:1 a & b)

Amen! And again, I say, *amen*!

CHAPTER 3

The Joy of Gay Scripture

If God had wanted Gays, He would have created Adam
and Steve, instead He created Adam and Eve.

First, let's set the record straight.

According to Jesus, God created male and female.

Matthew 19:4. "And He [Jesus] answered them and said unto
them, Have ye not read, that He which made them at the beginning
made them male and female?"

In the Scripture, whenever a person goes through a big psy-
chological and physical change, their name is changed: female to
Woman, Abram to Abraham, Sarai to Sarah, Saul to Paul, etc.

Male evolved into Adam.

Female evolved into Woman as soon as she married Adam, and
they had sex. She had lost her virginity and was physically changed.

If you will notice, nowhere does it mention that Woman was
fertile. There was no need to produce children. When they had eaten
of the tree of eternal life, they would have ceased to age and would
live forever at the age at which they had eaten of the tree.

So there they were perfect human beings in paradise, free to
make love any time they wanted, without the fear of pregnancy. In
essence, they were Adam and Steve, having sex without any hope of
children.

If the reader will recall, Adam and Woman were given three simple tasks: (1) tend the garden, (2) do not eat of the tree of the knowledge of good and evil, and (3) walk and talk with God in the cool of the evening. Three simple rules! And yet they so bungled up Eden that they managed to get everyone kicked out of paradise.

And if you will please note there was no gay person there at all.

But being cast out of the garden meant that they no longer had access to the tree of eternal life. In other words, death became a reality. That is why God opened up Woman's womb, and she became Eve—"mother of all living." Their task now was to reproduce the human race, feed it, clothe it, and raise it.

It's ironic that everyone talks about what Adam and Eve lost when they were cast out of paradise, but no one talks about what God lost that day.

He lost the very creatures he had created to love and serve him of their own free will. He had lost them to sin. Now they had to turn their attention to their offspring, which demanded all their time and energy.

That is why He created gay people and took away from us the drive to procreate. He is hoping that we will turn our time, money, and energy into worshiping Him of our own free will.

We are, in essence, Edenic Levites, very similar to the tribe of Levites who were assimilated into the Jews. It was their job to tend to the holy things of the tabernacle. It is our job to attend to the holy things of God.

He has given us three simple tasks to do: (1) honor His Sabbaths, (2) choose the things that please Him, and (3) take hold of His covenant.

But the reader might ask, "How can we do that when we're condemned in the Bible?"

It's a common misconception that gay people are condemned in the Bible. This belief was first proposed by Urban II in an attempt to make sure there would always be the next generation of pudgy little hands, dropping coins into the collection plate.

He chose three verses out of the Old Testament to back up his claim.

Thou shalt not lie with mankind, as with
womankind: it is abomination. (Leviticus 18:22)

If a man also lies with mankind, as he lieth
with a woman, both of them have committed an
abomination. (Leviticus 20:13)

Yes, that surely seems to condemn us until we stop and ask
ourselves: "When this was written, how did men lay with women?"

They treated women as their chattel property, like second-class
citizens to do with them whatever they desired. Take King Saul for
example. He treated Michal, his daughter, like she was his personal
property: first, she was pledged to one man, then given to David,
taken from David, and then given to Phalli. And David finally
claimed her as his property.

So then how is a man to lay with a man?

Each man is to be treated as an equal, not as a second-class citi-
zen. No matter what sexual position a man may take, he must still be
treated like a man—an equal.

Now the question arises: "Is there an example somewhere in the
Bible that proves that?" I think the marriage of David and Jonathan
proves that.

And he [Jonathan] said unto him [David]
Fear not for the hand of Saul my father shall not
find thee; and thou shalt be king over Israel, and
I shall be next to thee. (1 Samuel 23:17)

As to the third verse that supposedly condemns us, it's located
in Deuteronomy 23:17–18: "There shall be no whore of the daugh-
ters of Israel, nor a sodomite of the sons of Israel. Thou shall not
bring the hire of a whore, or the price of a dog into the house of the
Lord thy God for any vow: for even both these are abomination unto
the Lord thy God."

I always like looking at those Greek and Roman temples with
their pristine marble pillars. But I have often wondered just how

were they paid for? And where did the money come from to maintain all the priests and priestesses?

Public donations, of course, paid for some of it. Perhaps even the government paid for some of it. But there was always a whore-house connected to the temple. There you could get any kind of sex you wanted, as long as you had the money to pay for it. And the redeeming aspect of this was that you were doing it in the name of the god of that particular temple.

So we gay people better not follow false gods or prostitute ourselves. God considers it an abomination.

But we don't have to follow false gods. We gay people have our own covenant right out of the book of Isaiah.

> Neither let the eunuch [gay person] say, Behold I am a dry tree. For thus saith the Lord unto the eunuchs [gay people] that keep my Sabbaths, and choose the things that please me, and take hold of my covenant; even unto them will I give in mine house and within my walls a place and a name better than of sons and of daughters: I will give them an everlasting name, that shall not be cut off. (Isaiah 56:3–b, 4 & 5)

So as Adam was to dress and keep the Garden of Eden, we gay people must honor God's Sabbaths. As Adam was to please God by not eating of the tree of the knowledge of good and evil, so we must choose the things that please God. And finally, as Adam was to walk and talk with God in the evening, we gay people are to take hold of His covenant.

So how are we to please God?

Saint Paul writes in Hebrews 11:6, "But without faith it is impossible to please Him: for he that cometh to God must believe that He is, and that He is a rewarder of them who diligently seek Him."

So if we have faith in our God, would it not follow, like night follows day, that we would take the covenant that God has just given us?

What a joyous promise!

CHAPTER 4

The Joy of Gay Friendship

> And Ruth said, Entreat me not to leave thee or to return
> from following after thee: for wither thou goest, I will go;
> and where thou lodges! I will lodge: thy people shall be
> my people, and thy God, my God: Where thou diest, will
> I die, and there will I be buried: the Lord do so to me,
> and more also, if ought but death part me and thee.
>
> —Ruth 1:16–17

The story of Ruth is quite extraordinary. It is told in the book of the Bible called Ruth.

In the day of judges—of which time, no one is really quite certain—there arose a famine in Israel. So Elimelech, his wife Naomi, and his two sons Mahlon and Chilion moved from Bethlehem and settled in Moab.

While there, Elimelech died and left Naomi with her two sons.

Each of the sons married Moabite women, Orpah and Ruth. This means that they married outside of the Jewish faith. But apparently, they lived together in a straight existence for a good ten years according to the Bible. They were a very close-knit family—but no children.

Then both Mahlon and Chilion died, leaving Naomi alone with her two daughters-in-law.

Naomi decided to return to Bethlehem, having nothing more in Moab to hold her there. And her two daughters-in-law followed her.

But on the way, Naomi stopped, gave each daughter-in-law a kiss on the cheek, and told both of them to go back to Moab and find themselves husbands.

At first, the two women wept and would not leave her, saying, "Surely we will return with thee unto thy people."

Naomi again admonished them to return to Moab and find husbands. And again, both Orpah and Ruth wept.

Orpah then turned around and went back to Moab. But Ruth *cleaved* to Naomi.

It was then that Ruth said those beautiful, cherished words of love, which I quoted at the beginning of the chapter.

> And Ruth said, Entreat me not to leave thee or to return from following after thee: for wither thou goest, I will go; and where thou lodges! I will lodge: thy people shall be my people, and thy God, my God: Where thou diest, will I die, and there will I be buried: the Lord do so to me, and more also, if ought but death part me and thee. (Ruth 1:16–17)

They had become *super sisters*, much like *blood brothers*.
Were they Lesbians?
Only they knew.

There is a phenomenon in the male straight world that is known as *blood brothers*. In such a relationship, both men, though straight, pledge themselves to each other. This is portrayed many times in literature and movies and even in the Bible.

> And there is a friend that sticketh closer than a brother. (Proverbs 18:24)

A few examples to cite are the characters of Laurel and Hardy comedy. Or take the Abbott and Costello movies. And the Lone Ranger certainly had his Tonto.

Returning to the story of Ruth, these two women were straight, having both been married to their husbands and, if the author would assume, very happily so.

Naomi and Ruth returned to Bethlehem, Naomi's birthplace.

Unfortunately, Naomi complained that God had done her wrong, leaving her with no offspring.

And she repeated it several times. (Don't forget—the two sons she did have died in Moab.)

After the two women returned to Bethlehem, Ruth started gleaning for extra grain that the reapers had overlooked in a field owned by a man named Boaz.

Boaz spotted her and was instantly captivated by her. (Love at first sight?) So much so that he invited her to sit with him and the reapers and have lunch.

In fact, he told his reapers to leave some extra grain deliberately for Ruth to glean. When Naomi heard of this, she quickly devised a plot to get Ruth married to Boaz.

After a rather healthy feasting and drinking bout, Boaz stretched out on the threshing floor. Ruth, after midnight, came and lay beside him while he was sleeping.

Suddenly, he woke up and discovered Ruth lying beside him.

When he asked who she was, she replied, "Ruth, a near kinsman of yours," and asked Boaz to take her under his protection. Boaz praised her for not running after young men, thereby implying that he was several years older than she. And he said that he would provide protection.

He then reminded her that there was a nearer kinsman to her than him and that he would have the first claim on her.

After a rather convincing argument, the nearer kinsman relinquished his claim to Ruth. And so Boaz bought her from the other kinsman.

Ruth then became Boaz's wife. He knew her, and she conceived Obed.

Naomi, as any grandmother would, paraded her new grandchild all around town, praising God for giving her offspring. So she had a chance to live vicariously through Ruth.

But the reader might ask at this point, "Yes, that's a very nice story, but what does that have to do with the joy of being gay?"

According to the Scripture, Boaz (through Ruth, a Moabitess) begat Obed. And Obed begat Jesse, and Jesse begat David.

> And he [Jesse] sent, and brought him [David] in. Now he was ruddy, and withal of a beautiful countenance and goodly to look to. (1 Samuel 16:12)

As we shall see in a later chapter, David was quite good-looking with a healthy and rosy pink complexion.

In other words, the extra genes that Ruth brought in from Moab showed themselves in the next few generations.

There might also have been a gay gene because even though David had eight wives and produced children, he himself admitted to his gayness.

As the story unfolds in subsequent chapters, the reader will see how important the friendship of the super sisters had to be.

Without that intense friendship, Ruth would have returned to Moab as her sister-in-law Orpah did, carrying her genes with her. There would have been no David, no Davidic line, and eventually no Jesus.

It took those rogue genes to begin the line of David. And from that line, Jesus had to come, bringing salvation to the whole human race.

Certainly that should be considered joyous.

CHAPTER 5

The Joy of Being a Single Gay Person

Considering the many people listed in the Bible, are there any single gay men in there?

Yes, there are three who we can conclude are gay.

How do we know they were gay? There are several ways we can tell.

First of all, if the Bible says he's gay, then we can conclude he's gay. We're not about to argue with God's Holy Word.

If he says he's Gay, we will accept that at face value. Certainly, the man should surely know his own sexual orientation.

And finally, the last way to tell he's gay is if he fulfills three conditions: (1) Is there a physical description of him in the Bible? (For example, we have no idea how Matthew, Mark, Luke, or John looked like.) (2) Is he in an openly gay situation? (3) Are there words such as *tender love, beloved,* or *dearly beloved* used in relation to him?

Let us examine the three single men in the Bible. The first one we encounter is Daniel.

The Bible tells us that Daniel was extremely good-looking and intelligent. That is why he was taken to Babylon as a prisoner.

> And the king (Nebuchadnezzar) spake unto Ashpenaz the master of his eunuchs, that he should bring certain of the children [youths] of Israel, and of the king's seed, and of the princes;

children in whom was no blemish, but well favored, and skillful in all wisdom, and cunning in knowledge, and understanding science, and such as had ability in them to stand in the king's palace, and whom they might teach the learning and the tongue of the Chaldeans. (Daniel 1:3–4)

There is another reference to his good looks by Daniel himself.

Therefore I was left alone, and saw the great vision, and there remained no strength in me; for my comeliness was turned in me into corruption, and I retained no strength. (Daniel 10:8)

Was he in an openly gay situation?

As a young man reading the Bible, I often wondered how Daniel got away with the things he did. He was a prisoner of war. Yet look at what he demanded.

And Daniel purposed in his heart that he would not defile himself with the portion of the king's meat, nor with the wine which he drank. (Daniel 1:8)

He also worshiped Jehovah instead of the pagan gods.

Any other prisoner of war who did those things would quickly be thrown in the dungeon, tortured, or even executed.

So how did Daniel get away with it?

Now God brought Daniel into favor and tender love with the prince of the eunuchs. (Daniel 1:9)

In other words, Daniel was having a love affair with Ashpenaz, the head of the eunuchs.

Now concerning the last requirement, Daniel is referred to as "beloved" in two different places: Daniel 9:23 and Daniel 10:11.

It's a safe bet Daniel was castrated because he didn't return to Jerusalem to help rebuild the temple with either Ezra or Nehemiah.

> He that is wounded in the stones or hath
> his privy member cut off shall not enter into the
> congregation of the Lord. (Deuteronomy 23:1)

But even that didn't stop him from worshiping the Lord. Three times a day, he would open his window toward Jerusalem and pray to his God, thanking him.

The second gay man we will look at is Saint Paul.

Does he fit our requirements to determine gayness?

Is there a physical description of him?

Let us look at first what Lockyer says in his book *All The Men In The Bible* © 1957 Zondervan, p. 270.

> Paul's bodily size and appearance may have
> been against him, judging from a second century
> apocryphal description of him: 'He was a man
> little of stature, partly bald, with crooked legs,
> a vigorous physique, with eyes set close together
> and nose somewhat hooked.'

Saint Paul seems to agree with that description when he writes in 2 Corinthians 10:10: "For his letters, say they, are weighty and powerful: but his bodily presence is weak, and his speech contemptible."

There is one thing that we can all agree on—he was by no means good-looking. Now the question arises: was he in an obviously gay situation?

Yes, he was.

When the early Christian church started out, there was a controversy between Saint Paul and Saint Peter over what new Christians should and shouldn't do.

One example was circumcision.

Saint Peter contended that the new convert, following the Jewish tradition, had to be circumcised.

Saint Paul disagreed, saying that Christians were not under the old Jewish law.

But then, why did he circumcise Timothy?

> Him [Timothy] would Paul have to go forth
> with him; and took and circumcised him because
> of the Jews which were in those quarters: for they
> all knew his father was a Greek. (Acts 16:3)

Did he circumcise Timothy to appease the Jews in the city? Or did he just want to *check* Timothy out, so to speak?

I guess we'll never know.

One thing is very clear though.

Saint Paul abhorred his own homosexuality.

> And lest I should be exalted above mea-
> sure through the abundance of the revelations,
> there was given to me a thorn in the flesh, the
> messenger of Satan to buffet me, lest I should be
> exalted above measure. For this thing I besought
> the Lord therein that it might depart from me.
> And he said unto me, My grace is sufficient for
> thee: for my strength is made perfect in weak-
> ness. Most gladly therefore will I rather glory in
> my infirmities, that the power of Christ may rest
> upon me. (2 Corinthians 12:7–9)

Most theologians think that the *thorn* in his flesh was his homosexuality.

Unfortunately, all too many men, like Saint Paul, pray that their gayness be taken away from them, not realizing the blessings God wants to give them. Unfortunately also, all too many of them don't read their Bible because they think, wrongly, that they are condemned in there.

Perhaps this handbook can inspire them to read about God's holy plan for his gay people. Now did Saint Paul use such words as *beloved* and *dearly beloved*?

I think a few examples should answer that question.

"Greet Amplias my beloved in the Lord" (Romans 16:8). *Amplias*, according to Lockyer, means "enlarged," (p. 42).

Isn't that interesting?

> Paul, an apostle of Jesus Christ by the will of God, according to the promise of life which is in Christ Jesus, to Timothy, my dearly beloved son. (2 Timothy 1:1–2)

> Paul, a prisoner of Jesus Christ, and Timothy our brother unto Philemon, our dearly beloved and fellow laborer. (Philemon 1:1)

I think that proves my point.

Now let us pass on to the last gay man in the Bible who we know of.

His story is found in the book of Acts 8:26–40.

The passage is far too long to quote here so we will have to do with a summary.

An angel of the Lord told Philip "the preacher" to go into the desert and wait.

While he was there, a caravan passed by that included an Ethiopian eunuch in his chariot, returning from worshiping in Jerusalem. While he was traveling, he was reading from the book of Isaiah.

The angel told Philip to go to the eunuch's chariot and talk to him.

Philip then ran (please note—ran) to the chariot and began talking to him, converting him to Christianity.

The eunuch asked to be baptized.

Somehow they found water in the desert, and Philip baptized him. After that, the eunuch went on his way, rejoicing, and passed into history. Philip, having done the angel's bidding, was whisked away. Now how do we know that the Ethiopian eunuch was gay?

Scripture tells us that the man was returning to Ethiopia from worshiping in Jerusalem. And at that time, there was only one place to worship in Jerusalem—the temple.

But physically castrated men weren't allowed into the temple. (See Deuteronomy 23:1.)

Someone suggested that he was relegated to the woman's court.

A very important man like he was? It would have created an international incident.

As we have found *eunuch* may also be interpreted as gay person (J. J. McNeil, *The Church and the Homosexual*, p. 64 Beacon Press; *All the Trades and Occupations of the Bible*, Lockyer, definition of *eunuch*).

And in this case, we think the interpretation fits.

What was he reading from the Book of Isaiah?

The Scripture that foretold the gay messiah.

Coincidence?

I don't think so.

So now we have a gay black man.

How do we know he was black?

Living in an interracial country, we sometimes forget that some countries are all one race.

Ethiopia is one. The nation is all black. Therefore, the Ethiopian eunuch was a gay black man There may be more single gay people in the Bible, but we must be careful that we don't go on a witch hunt.

Are there any lessons that can be learned from these three men?

First of all, they were all educated and intelligent: Daniel was chosen for his looks and intelligence, Saint Paul bragged that he was taught by Gamaliel, a leading teacher of his time, and the gay black man was the head of Candace, the queen's treasury, a very prestigious position, which obviously required a great deal of intelligence.

Saint Paul himself urges Christians to get an education.

Study to shew thyself approved unto God, a
workman that needeth not to be ashamed rightly
dividing the word of truth. (2 Timothy 2:15)

Daniel worked well within the system under four different kings—Nebuchadnezzar, Belshazzar, Darius, and Cyrus. The gay black man obviously worked well, also, within the system.

Saint Paul worked well outside of the system, setting up Christian churches wherever he could, defying the old pagan religions.

In their own special way, each of them dealt with their gayness. And all of them worshiped the same God.

I like to think of them as the three Bs—the beauty, the butch, and the black man.

CHAPTER 6

The Joy of a Two-Career Gay Marriage

> I am distressed for thee, my brother Jonathan. Very
> pleasant hast thou been unto me: thy love to me
> was wonderful, passing the love of women.
> —2 Samuel 1:26

Such beautiful words of David.

But who was David? Or Jonathan, for that matter?

David was the eighth son of Jesse. We don't know what Jesse did for a living. But we do know David was keeping the sheep. So apparently, Jesse was a farmer of sorts.

Why was David important?

It seems King Saul had displeased the Lord by not following His commandments. So the Lord sent the prophet Samuel down to Bethlehem to anoint a new king. And He led him to the house of Jesse.

After looking at the older seven brothers, the Lord chose David to be the newly anointed king over Israel.

But the old king didn't know this. Once when he was feeling sad and melancholy, one of his men suggested David, who was known to play the harp quite well, come and play for him.

So then he would have David come and play for him whenever he felt sad. In fact, Saul liked him so well that he made him his armor-bearer.

Everyone, I'm sure, is familiar with the story of David and Goliath. How the Philistines put Goliath up to a one-to-one battle against any one of the Israeli men, none of whom would take the challenge.

But David came forward.

At first, King Saul dressed David in all the armor he had. But it wouldn't work.

David took all the armor off, took his slingshot and five small pebbles from a nearby stream, and faced the giant.

Goliath looked down at the young David and openly disdained him.

But that didn't deter David one bit. He stood there, assessed the situation, and then swung his slingshot with a pebble in it.

The stone landed right between Goliath's eyes and instantly killed him.

David was brought before the king who amply rewarded him for his bravery and cunning. It was right after the interview with Saul that David met Jonathan.

It was love at first sight!

> And it came to pass, when he had made an end
> of speaking unto Saul that the soul of Johnathan
> was knit with the soul of David, and Jonathan
> loved him as his own soul. (1 Samuel 18:4)

Now the question comes up: Who was Jonathan? Jonathan was the oldest of King Saul's children.

It's amazing that they had never met before with David's coming and going in and out of the court.

Most of the time, however, David spent his time keeping sheep in the field and practicing with his slingshot and harp.

Jonathan, meanwhile, was busy practicing his military skills. They loved each other so much that they were married.

> So Jonathan made a covenant with the
> house of David, saying, Let the Lord even require

it at the hands of David's enemies. And Jonathan
caused David to swear again, because he loved
him. For he loved him as his own soul. (1 Samuel
20:16–17)

How do we know this wasn't just a *blood brother* situation?
Because the Bible tells us that they consummated their marriage.

And as soon as the lad was gone, David
arose out of a place toward the south, and fell on
his face to the ground, and bowed himself three
times: and they kissed one another, and wept one
with another until David exceeded. (1 Samuel
20:41)

Exceeded is the old English word for *climaxed*.
Did they follow the law and treat each other as equals?

And thou [David] shalt be king over Israel,
and I [Jonathan] shall be next to thee; and that
also Saul my father knoweth. (1 Samuel 23:17)

The man who gave his kingdom up for the man he loved was
going to be with David as he sat on the throne. They were both going
to be as equal as they could be.

To understand the importance of this marriage, we first have to
consider just where Israel was situated.

It was situated along the eastern Mediterranean coastline, which
made it a very strategic spot. It was below Babylonia and above Egypt.

Merchants had three options for shipping their goods: (1) They
could load their goods on ships and sail up and down the coast.
Because of the pirates constantly roaming the seas that was a very bad
idea. The ships could be hijacked. (2) They could load their wares
on camels and go through the Negev desert. This was a bad idea too.
The heat was so intense that being in the desert could very quickly

mean death. (3) They could load up their camels and go along the land routes, which was the safest bet.

That means that those land routes would go right straight through Israel. And whoever controlled those routes could tax the caravans as much as they liked.

And, of course, they did. Solomon, for example, grew extremely wealthy by those taxes. Some of those caravans could have five hundred to one thousand camels. So even if he charged—say, a shekel a camel—and with caravans going up and down the coast every day, he was constantly making a lot of money.

As we have already seen, Saul was king.

However, the Lord told Samuel, his prophet, to anoint David as the new king. All well and good.

But unfortunately, the old king wouldn't go away.

In fact, he declared David to be an outlaw and set out to hunt him down and kill him. David had to go on the run.

But what would have happened if Saul would have died?

There would have been a devastating civil war between Jonathan, who had a right to the throne by ascension, and David, who had the same right to the throne by anointing.

The enemies of Israel were just waiting at the gate, so to speak, for this to happen so that they could move in and take command of those very valuable trade routes.

But by uniting the house of Jonathan with that of David in gay marriage, the situation resolved itself.

So David was able to start the Davidic line from which the Messiah was to come.

Yes, David had eight wives and produced children. But as he said, his heart just wasn't in it.

> I am distressed for thee my brother Jonathan.
> Very pleasant hast thou been unto me: thy love to
> me was wonderful, passing the love of women. (2
> Samuel 1:26)

CHAPTER 7

The Joy of a Nurturer/Provider Gay Marriage

When Jesus therefore saw his mother, and the disciple standing by whom he loved, he saith unto his mother, Woman, behold thy son! Then he saith unto the disciple, Behold thy mother! And from that hour that disciple took her unto his own home.
—John 19:26

Was the union between Jesus and Saint John a gay marriage?
First, let us look at what prophecy has to say about it.
We will start with the prophecy of the *provider*.

> Who hath believed our report? And to whom is the arm of the Lord revealed? For he shall grow up before him as a tender plant, and as a root out of a dry ground: he hath no form nor comeliness: and when we shall see him, there is not beauty that we should desire him. (Isaiah 53:1–2)

Even the prophet has to ask, "Who is going to believe this?" It is rather hard to believe.

From what Isaiah says, the Messiah is to come from very lowly beginnings.

The prophet also tells us that the man will not be good-looking at all, lest we be led astray by his looks.

But why would the prophet comment on the Messiah's lack of good looks? To a straight man, another man's good looks would hardly stir desire in him. But it might very well sway someone who is gay. Obviously, the author is talking about an openly gay situation.

It's a very open statement, and I accept it at face value.

Now let us turn our attention to the *nurturer*.

A lot of people think that the fifty-fourth chapter of Isaiah represents the spiritual church. And in a sense, it does.

But as the prophecies will prove, the prophet means a real person.

In Isaiah, the prophet gives us six prophecies, concerning the *nurturer*.

First, we are told that the *nurturer* will have no physical children. But in the same verse (Isaiah 54:1), the prophet seemingly contradicts himself by saying that the person will have many children.

Second, those children of this person who has no children will cause deserted cities to be inhabited (Isaiah 54:3). Third, this person will actually be married to the Messiah.

> For thy Maker is thine husband, the Lord
> of Hosts is his name: and thy redeemer the Holy
> One of Israel; and God of the whole earth shall
> he be called. (Isaiah 54:5)

Fourth, the provider will be upset with the *nurturer* but will soon patch things up with him (Isaiah 54:8).

Fifth, all those none children shall be taught of the Lord (Isaiah 54:13). And sixth, the *nurturer* will never be martyred (Isaiah 54:17).

Was Jesus the Messiah?

If he were, then he would have to fulfill all the prophecies concerning the Messiah.

We are assured that Jesus fulfilled prophecy many times in the Gospels, too many to quote here. But let us take a look at Isaiah's prophecy.

First, we know he was born in Bethlehem. And Bethlehem was hardly a thriving commercial center. Rather it was a sleepy, country kind of town.

Was Jesus good-looking or not?

We have no real description of him. But considering the many times we're told Jesus fulfilled prophecy, we can safely consider the man was hardly good-looking as many artists portray him.

We know that there is a large gap in Jesus's history. Where he went and what he experienced we can only guess.

But he brought his teachings and wisdom back to share with us.

Even so, he couldn't escape the stigma of being a lowly carpenter in his own town.

> Is this not the carpenter's son? Is not his mother called Mary. (Matthew 13:55)

It was he who coined the term "no prophet is honored in his own country."

We can conclude if Jesus was the Messiah, then he had to be gay and be married gay. Was he married? And if so, to whom?

Of all of the dozens of people mentioned in the New Testament, there is only one who fits all the prophecies. He was Saint John.

All of the disciples were married straight except for Saint John. So Saint John did not sire any physical children, which is what the prophet said.

So how could Saint John have children when he was childless?

Saint John considered new believers his children and said so. In his three short letters in the Bible, he refers to new believers as his "little children."

This fulfills the first prophecy. And it also fulfills the fifth prophecy that the children shall be taught of the Lord.

In the second prophecy, Isaiah said that those none children (new believers) will cause deserted cities to be inhabited. When Saint John was convicted of not worshiping Roman gods, he was sentenced to be exiled to the isle of Patmos, which was a lonely little island in the ocean. There was a small port there and Saint John's hut.

When Nero died, Saint John was released and returned to Ephesus where he preached and taught the newcomers until his death, thus fulfilling the sixth prophecy.

The island was completely deserted.

Now there is a thriving seaport there and a monastery where Saint John's shack stood. He had fulfilled prophecy again.

Was Saint John married to Jesus?

> When Jesus therefore saw his mother, and the disciple standing by whom he loved, he saith unto his mother, Woman, behold thy son! Then he saith unto the disciple, Behold thy mother! And from that hour that disciple took her unto his own home. (John 19:26–27)

In other words, Jesus raised his relationship with John to that of a biological family and told Mary to regard Saint John as her son-in-law.

There was only one time Jesus was upset with Saint John and his brother Saint James. And that was when Saint John and Saint James were arguing over how high their place in heaven would be (Matthew 20:20–23).

He reminded them and their mother, who was trying to advocate for them, that it was not his place to say. He was upset at their mother and the two men for asking.

But he quickly got over it.

What makes this marriage important?

If Jesus was going to be the Messiah, then he had to fulfill all the messianic prophecies, including being gay and being married gay.

Being the Messiah, he brought salvation to the entire world! And that is a very joyous thing!

CHAPTER 8

The Joy of Psalm 133 "In Praise of Gay Marriage"

Behold how good and how pleasant it is for brethren to dwell together in harmony. It is like the precious ointment upon the head, that ran down the beard, even Aaron's beard: that went down to the skirts of his garments: as the dew of Herman, and as the dew that descended upon the mountains of Zion: for there the Lord commanded the blessings, even life for evermore.

—Psalm 133:

What makes this psalm in praise of gay marriage?

According to John Boswell in his book *Same-Sex Unions in Premodem Europe* (Villard 1994), Saints Serge and Bacchus of the early Christian church used it to justify their gay marriage.

Were they correct in doing so?

Is there any example in the Bible that can be used to show *brother* or *brethren* can be translated as gay lovers?

Yes, there is.

If you will recall in chapter 5, I quoted 2 Samuel 1:26, which I will quote again here: "I am distressed for thee my brother Jonathan. Very pleasant hast thou been unto me: thy love to me was wonderful, passing the love of women."

In fact, carrying that reasoning even further we can say, in many cases, unless the term *brethren* is not specifically qualified biologically—it can be interpreted to be gay lovers.

Is there any other place in the Bible we can make the same distinction?

Yes, there is.

> If brethren dwell together and one of them die, and have no child, the wife of the dead shall not marry without unto a stranger: her husband's brother shall go in unto her, and take her to him to wife, and perform the duty of a husband's brother unto her. (Deuteronomy 25:5)

This can hardly be considered biological brothers because of the passage in Leviticus.

> Thou shall not uncover the nakedness of thy brother's wife: it is thy bother's nakedness. (Leviticus 18:16)

Therefore, "brethren" must have a different meaning than biological siblings.

Don't forget, even though David had eight wives, he was still married to Jonathan.

Yet look how he compared his gay marriage as precious ointment—meaning something sacred. And to reinforce the meaning of *sacred*, he likened it to the ointment used on Aaron's head, the first high priest.

He further equates gay marriage to dew, which in the Bible stands for peace. To reinforce the holiness of this peace, he likened it to the dew on Mount Hermon and Mount Zion, both holy mountains. Saint Paul also comments on gay marriage in his letter to the Hebrews.

> Let brotherly love continue. (Hebrews 13:1)

Then in just two short verses, later he writes Hebrews 13:4, "Marriage is honorable in all, and the bed undefiled."

There are those who will scoff at our interpretation. There will be those who contest it. And there will be those who will completely ignore it.

But as Jesus said, this wasn't given to them. It was given to us.

What a joyous psalm it truly is!

CHAPTER 9

The Joyous Promise of a Gay Future

> Remember ye not the former things, neither consider
> the things of old. "Behold, I do a new thing; now it
> shall spring forth; shall ye not know it? I will even make
> a way in the wilderness, and rivers in the desert.
> —Isaiah 43:18

Coming out is a continuing process.

We must never forget that what we are dealing with is almost a thousand years of negative training started around 1075 by Urban II in the early Catholic church. What his motives were we can hardly guess. We can make some fairly accurate assumptions though.

But even if we could guess correctly as to what his motives were, we must heed the words of the prophet Isaiah and let go of the old, turn around, and face the future.

We must let go of the hurt and anger caused by our fellow human beings. They were only reflecting on what they have been taught. Considering that everything they have ever seen, everything they have ever heard, and everything they have ever read has been straight, with very little exception, it's not surprising that they think the way they do.

That is why we should be reminding the people around us that we are different from them. And we should celebrate that difference.

The first thing we must do is break this wall of silence.

It's okay to say you're gay right out in the open, even in church.

It may be shocking to a lot of people, but then again, they have been trained in believing that being gay is something to be ashamed of.

It's not!

Didn't David write a whole psalm in praise of gay marriage? He certainly wasn't ashamed of talking about his beloved Jonathan. And look how openly he lamented his husband's death.

> I am distressed for thee, my brother Jonathan: very pleasant hast thou been unto me: thy love to me was wonderful, passing the love of women. (2 Samuel 1:26)

Didn't Saint John in his book of the Bible intimate that he was the disciple whom Jesus loved? And he constantly repeated it throughout the whole book.

The people must be taught that there are gay people who never marry. Yet this doesn't stop them from being gay, even though they have never had a homosexual experience in their life.

Yet there are many gay people who marry and enjoy very full love life.

But we must never forget we are Christians, as well as gay. Then what are we to do as gay Christians?

Jesus said it quite plainly in Matthew 5:14–16,

> Ye are the light of the world. A city that is set on a hill cannot be hid. Neither do men light a candle, and put it under a bushel, but on a candlestick: and it giveth light unto all that are in the house. Let your light so shine before men, that they may see your good works, and glorify your Father which is in heaven.

We must develop our own Gay culture.

We can start by modifying the existing straight culture to reflect our own gay existence.

For example, there is a gay rodeo that takes place in Phoenix, Arizona. And there is a gay Olympics, although it's not called that anymore. It's called the Gay Games. Granted there are gay pride parades, but they only take place once a year.

On a more local level, how about gay folk dances? Gay square dancing? Gay hayrides?

What we must also do is to cultivate our gay musicians who sing and play about their gay experience, singing of their love for their husbands or lovers. And there must be no hiding this gay under a cloak of silence. How comforting it would be to hear some gay singer, singing about his newfound love or lamenting about his lost one.

We should start our own gay Nashville featuring new gay singers.

And don't forget about our gay artists, dancers, composers, and actors. We must do everything we can to encourage these gifted people. It is through them that we can explain the joyous gay experiences.

One important thing we must do is to have translators work on a gay translation of the Bible. The Bible we have-the standard King James Version—should be brought up to date.

We now have modem terms for the Gay existence.

There should be no more pussyfooting around with the old English expressions that try to explain the situation. They are so antiquated.

What we need is someone to look at the Bible through gay eyes, not restricted by social convention or laws.

For example, in the verse that tells us that David and Jonathan are making love, the Bible says: "Until David exceeded." *Exceeded* is an old English word for *climaxed*. Today, *climaxed* should be used. But unfortunately, it isn't.

In a larger sense, we must now look at the impact of gay existence on society.

It is a known fact that our planet is vastly overpopulated. With medical practices and medicines, more people are living longer—

much longer. Now combine that with fertility procedures to enhance childbirth, and a very deadly situation arises. There must be some way to cut the population size down.

And there is.

It is called gay life.

We are the natural check on the overpopulation problem. Mother Nature has already provided that check.

Unfortunately, human institutions have, for hundreds of years, tried to block Mother Nature and lay their own man-made laws over the population.

But thank goodness, this is changing—and changing very rapidly which is a very good thing.

That is why we must raise our gay multicolored flag and rejoice in our God-given gayness.

As we quoted before and must be quoted again and again in Matthew 5:14–16,

> Ye are the light of the world. A city that is set on a hill cannot be hid. Neither do men light a candle, and put it under a bushel, but on a candlestick: and it giveth light unto all that are in the house. Let your light so shine before men, that they may see your good works, and glorify your Father which is in heaven.

That is why we must rejoice and be exceedingly glad for our joyous existence.

ABOUT THE AUTHOR

I started my research into gay biblical theology in 1984 after being challenged by a Catholic priest. The more I researched, the more I was amazed at the wonderful blessings the Bible says God has for us gay people, and those blessings are ours. That is why we, Gay men, need never consider ourselves an abomination or useless. God loves us just the way we are.

www.ingramcontent.com/pod-product-compliance
Lightning Source LLC
Chambersburg PA
CBHW061230280526
45784CB00006B/2713